AF413374

Sprinkle Seeds *of* Kindness

Written by
Jessica Elkin

Illustrated by
Meredith Cole

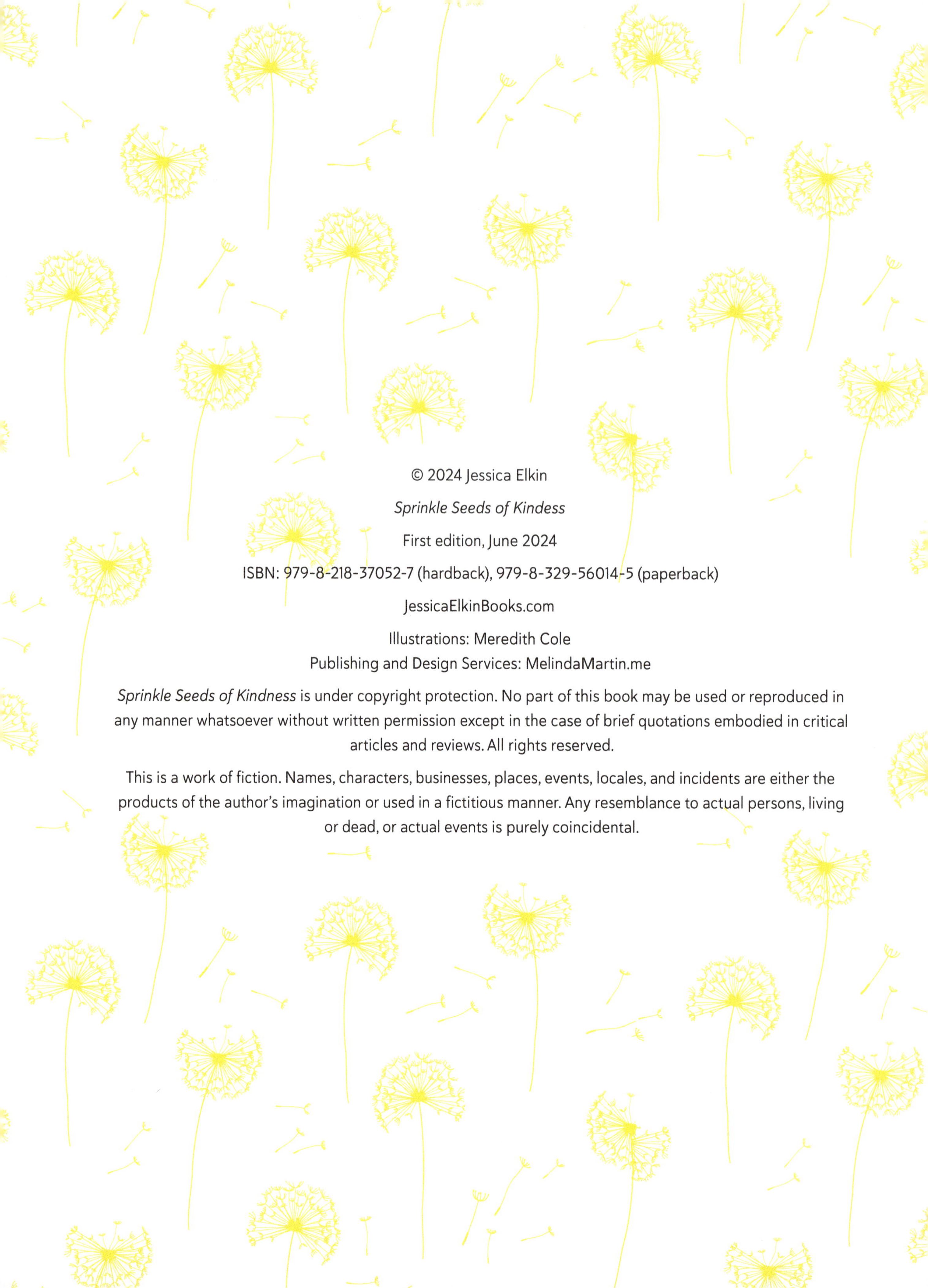

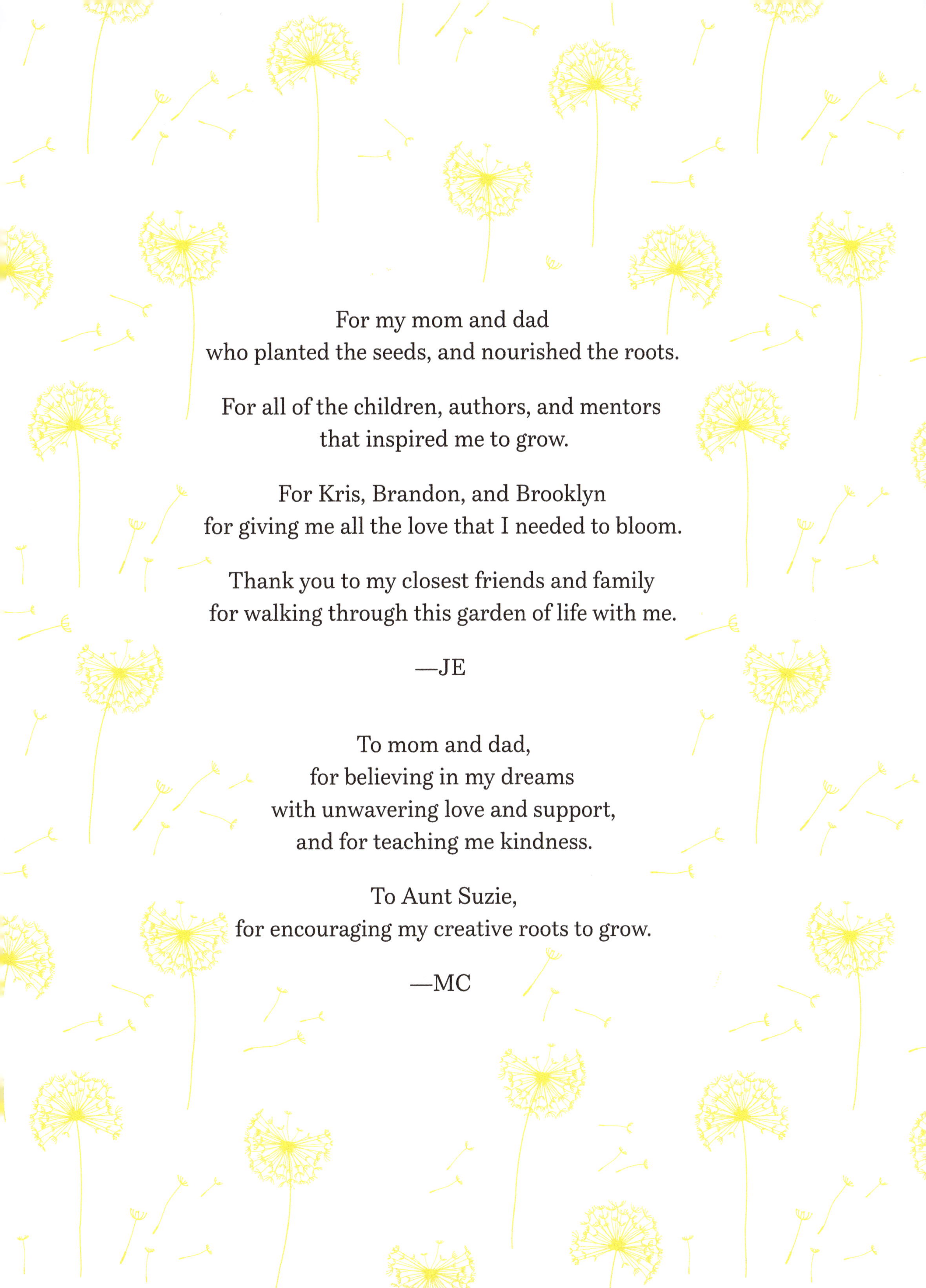

For my mom and dad
who planted the seeds, and nourished the roots.

For all of the children, authors, and mentors
that inspired me to grow.

For Kris, Brandon, and Brooklyn
for giving me all the love that I needed to bloom.

Thank you to my closest friends and family
for walking through this garden of life with me.

—JE

To mom and dad,
for believing in my dreams
with unwavering love and support,
and for teaching me kindness.

To Aunt Suzie,
for encouraging my creative roots to grow.

—MC

Plant tiny seeds of kindness,
scattered, or in a row.

seeds

The seeds will sprout,
the flowers bloom,
and others soon will know.

Sprinkle, scatter, pitter-patter.
Kindness seeds will grow!

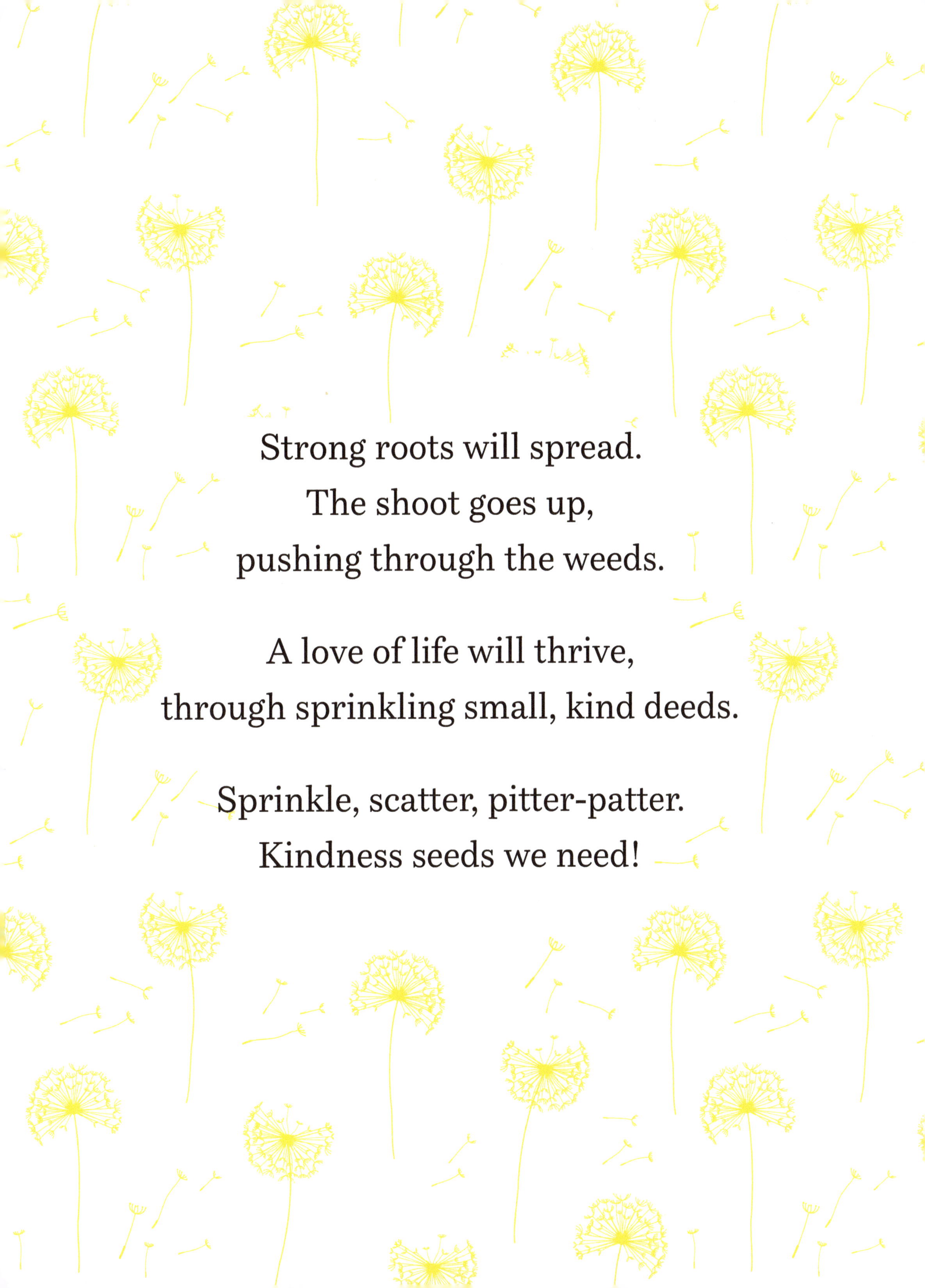

Strong roots will spread.
The shoot goes up,
pushing through the weeds.

A love of life will thrive,
through sprinkling small, kind deeds.

Sprinkle, scatter, pitter-patter.
Kindness seeds we need!

With someone old,
gather a crew.

Lend a hand
for someone new.

Sprinkle, scatter, pitter-patter.
Kindness seeds in view!

Choose someone bold,
gather a crowd.
Take a stand
and make it loud.

Sprinkle, scatter,
pitter-patter.
Kindness seeds
be proud!

In your school...

in your home...

in the world,
you're not alone.

Sprinkle, scatter, pitter-patter.
Kindness seeds be known!

Nourish yourself.
To you, be kind.

Fuel your body.
Calm your mind.

Sprinkle, scatter,
pitter-patter.

Kindness seeds
you'll find!

So, be the soil—
so strong;

sunlight
that's bright;

the rain coming down.

And soon others will sow,
sprinkling seeds of joy and love...

. . . watching as it grows.

Sunlight of loving kindness,
shining from above,

on fields of flowers
grown by these seeds...
and our love.

Sprinkle, scatter, pitter-patter.

Kindness seeds do matter!

Before Reading

- Read the title and ask: What do you think this book might be about? What do you notice on the cover that makes you think that? Look closely for all of the clues!

- What do you think a seed of kindness is?

During Reading

- What happened to her seeds? How is this like planting a seed of kindness? What happens to a seed of kindness after it is "planted"? Why are these children peeking over the fence? What are they noticing? Will they keep watching her? What might they do next?

- Why do we need kindness seeds?

- What are the children doing in their classroom to be kind? What else could they do? Have you ever done something kind in a classroom?

- What is the girl doing in her home to be kind? What else could she do? What have you done at home to be kind?

- Do seeds travel? Does kindness travel?

- What does it mean to nourish yourself? What is this girl doing for her body? Her mind? What could you do for your body and your mind?

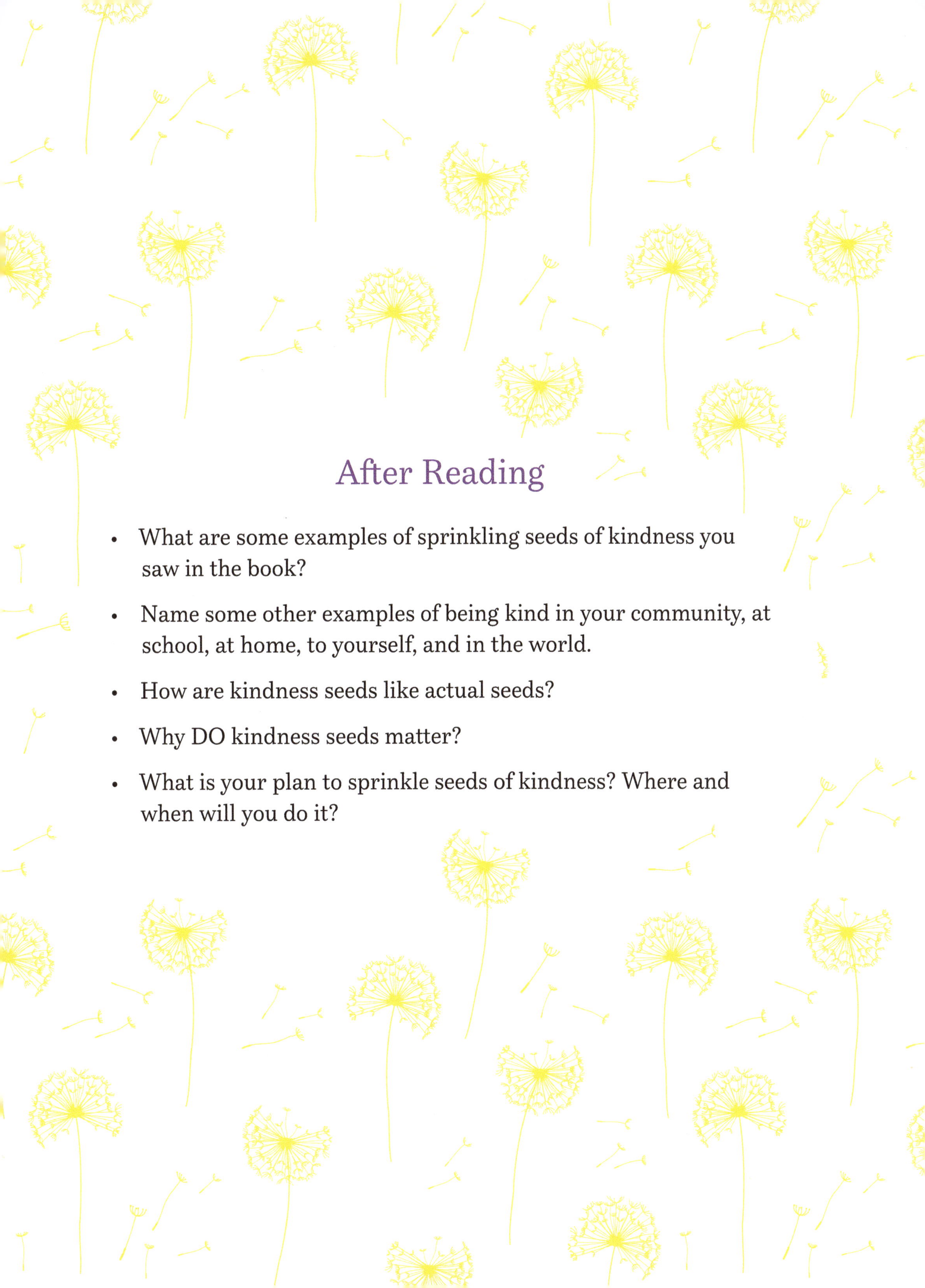

After Reading

- What are some examples of sprinkling seeds of kindness you saw in the book?

- Name some other examples of being kind in your community, at school, at home, to yourself, and in the world.

- How are kindness seeds like actual seeds?

- Why DO kindness seeds matter?

- What is your plan to sprinkle seeds of kindness? Where and when will you do it?

Plant a Seed of Kindess

Kindness Chain

Cut stripes of paper 1" wide by 8" long. Glue, tape, or staple the ends of the first strip together to form a loop. When you sprinkle kindness, or see someone else sprinkle kindness, add another loop, and watch the kindness grow! You might decide to write the kind act on the stripes, or create a paper flower to attach to the to loop!

Kindness Seeds Hunt

Go on a hunt through your other favorite stories in search of characters sprinkling kindness! Take 5-10 sticky notes and draw a heart on each one. Grab a stack of 3-5 of your favorite books, or check some out from the local library. As you read, find pictures, or words that are examples of sprinkling kindness. Share what you found with someone else so the kindness seeds can grow!

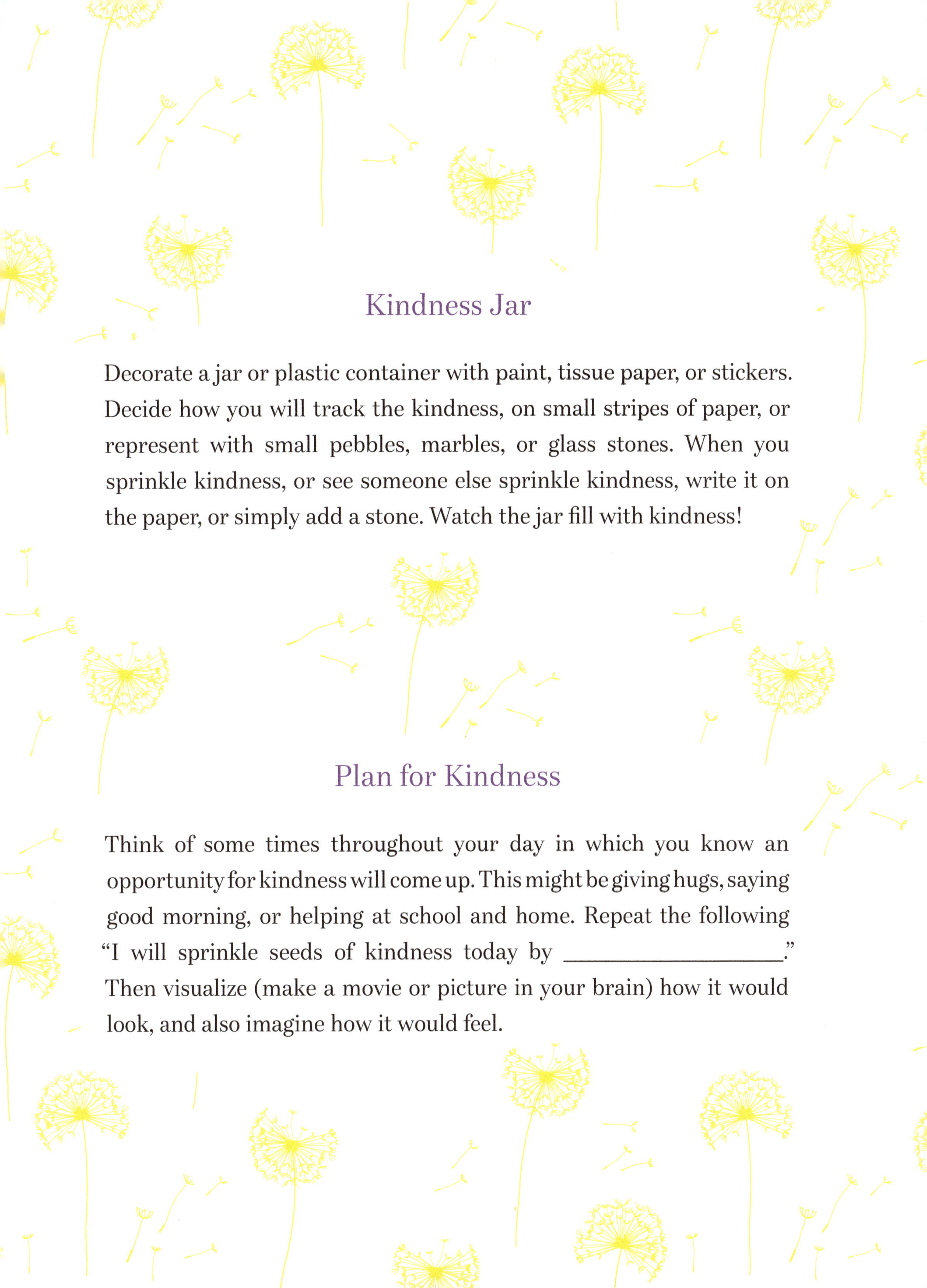

Kindness Jar

Decorate a jar or plastic container with paint, tissue paper, or stickers. Decide how you will track the kindness, on small stripes of paper, or represent with small pebbles, marbles, or glass stones. When you sprinkle kindness, or see someone else sprinkle kindness, write it on the paper, or simply add a stone. Watch the jar fill with kindness!

Plan for Kindness

Think of some times throughout your day in which you know an opportunity for kindness will come up. This might be giving hugs, saying good morning, or helping at school and home. Repeat the following "I will sprinkle seeds of kindness today by ___________________." Then visualize (make a movie or picture in your brain) how it would look, and also imagine how it would feel.

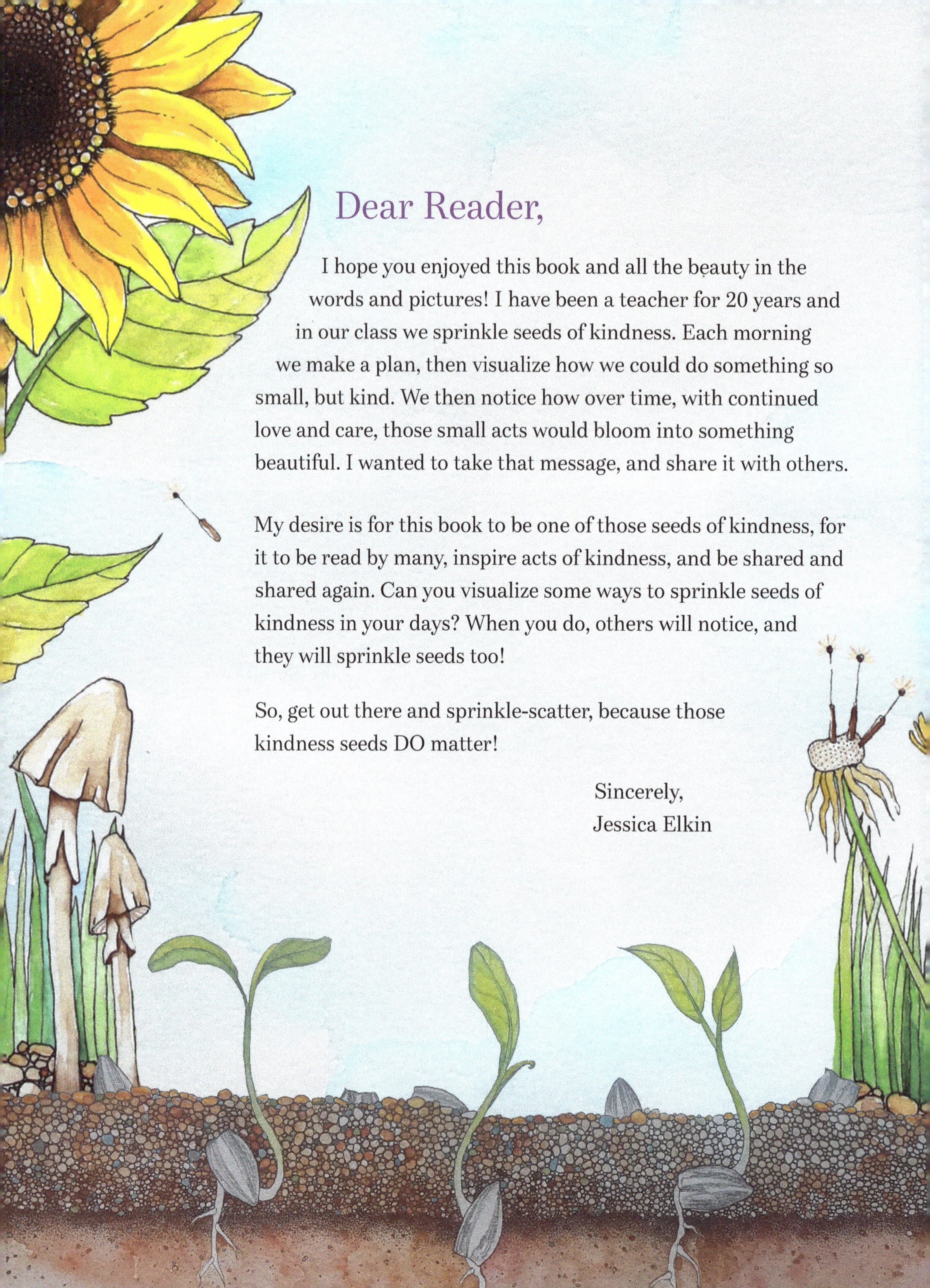

Dear Reader,

I hope you enjoyed this book and all the beauty in the
words and pictures! I have been a teacher for 20 years and
in our class we sprinkle seeds of kindness. Each morning
we make a plan, then visualize how we could do something so
small, but kind. We then notice how over time, with continued
love and care, those small acts would bloom into something
beautiful. I wanted to take that message, and share it with others.

My desire is for this book to be one of those seeds of kindness, for
it to be read by many, inspire acts of kindness, and be shared and
shared again. Can you visualize some ways to sprinkle seeds of
kindness in your days? When you do, others will notice, and
they will sprinkle seeds too!

So, get out there and sprinkle-scatter, because those
kindness seeds DO matter!

Sincerely,
Jessica Elkin

Jessica Elkin is a book enthusiast and teacher at heart. Jessica is a sower of kindness seeds. Many gardens she has grown in the form of "kinders" during her 20 years teaching Kindergarten through Second Grade. She has a passion for cultivating kindness, as well as growing young,enthusiastic writers. These experiences have allowed her to be completely immersed in the magic of Children's Literature and its powerful effects on children's learning. Sprinkle Seeds of Kindness is her first publication and was inspired by a special Kindergarten class, an inspiring author visit, and her lifelong passion to be an author. Jessica lives in Brighton, Michigan with her husband, her son, and her daughter. In her free time she can be found enjoying tacos, books, movies, and time with her family and friends.

Meredith Cole received her bachelor's degree in fine arts from the University of Michigan. This is her first time illustrating a children's book. She has been creating art since childhood. It is a reflection of her heart and soul. Her favorite medium to work in is drawing and watercolor painting. She is inspired by surrealism, human anatomy, nature, and emotion.

www.ingramcontent.com/pod-product-compliance
Lightning Source LLC
Chambersburg PA
CBHW040739150726
48196CB00011B/653